Swallowing Watermelons

Swallowing Watermelons

Karla Brundage

Ishmael Reed Publishing Company
Berkeley, California

Copyright © 2006 by Karla Brundage.
            First Printing

Library of Congress Control Number: 2006903848
ISBN :   Softcover   1-4257-1463-3

All rights reserved. No part of this book may be reproduced or transmitted in whole or in part without permission in writing from the author, Karla Brundage, or the publisher, Ishmael Reed, except for reviewers who may quote brief excerpts in connection with a review in a newspaper, magazine, or electronic publication; nor may any part of this book be reproduced, stored in a retrieval system, or transmitted in any form or by any means electronic, mechanical, photocopying, recording, or other, without written permission from the publisher or author.

Published in the United States of America by Ishmael Reed Publishing Company.

Some of the poems collected here have been previously published as follows:

        "Asha" appeared in *Hip Mama*, Fall, 1993.
    "Money" and "Lips" appeared in *Oahu Review*, 1997.
"Peaches" appeared in *Konch*, 1991; *Adam of Ife: Black Women in Praise of Black Men*, 1992; *La'iLa'i*, 1996.
"To Be a Man" appeared in *Adam of Ife: Black Women in Praise of Black Men*, 1992.
"Wanna Be White Girl," "Salt and Black Pepper," and "Great Grandmother Maud" appeared in *Intersecting Circles: Voices of Hapa Women in Poetry and Prose*, 1999.
        "Womb Dancing" appeared in *Hip Mama*, Fall, 1994.
    "Getting Ready for the Worst" appeared in *Hip Mama*, 2006.

        Please address all inquiries to:
        Ishmael Reed Publishing Co.
           P.O. Box 3288
       Berkeley, California 94703

          Cover Art: Audrey Driver
       Author Photo: Kathy Sloane

To order additional copies of this book, contact:
Xlibris Corporation
1-888-795-4274
www.Xlibris.com
Orders@Xlibris.com

CONTENTS

Acknowledgements   11

Part I

Muse	15
He Said . . . She Said	16
Pussy Controller	17
I Have Nowhere to put this Sorrow	20
Naked to the Party	21
Hate = Love (in rhyme)	23
Love = Hate (or silence wins)	25
Money	27
Welfare Queen	28
Black Woman's Dilemma	29
No Time for Cafés	31
Swallowing Watermelons	32
Resurrection I	33
Resurrection II	34

Part II

Orgasm in Haiku	37
Peaches	38
To Be a Man	40
Biking the Bay	41
Sweet Talker	42
Memoirs (self-restraint of a fallen virgin)	43
Lips	47
Eating a Tomato	49

Part III

Red Haired Sister in Full Fury	53
Red Haired Sister—My Beloved	54
The Last Time I Cried	55
Epilepsy	56

After the First Seizure	58
Car Accident	61

Part IV

Premonition	69
Competition of the Hair	70
Breasts	72
Great Grandmother Maud	74
Wanna Be White Girl	77
Dating the Oppressor	81
Ogun: New Year's Eve 2000	83
Womb Dancing	85
Asha	86
Getting Ready for the Worst	88
He Said	90
Whore She Is (Not)	91
Whore'song	93
Expecting Heaven	94
Peas in a Pod	96
Salt and Black Pepper	97
To Set Me Free	101
About the author	103

For Lottie and Maud

Poem Forty
by Rumi

Don't hide your heart but reveal it,
so that mine might be revealed,
and I might accept what I am capable of.

Mathnawi 1, 2682

Acknowledgements

This book would not have been possible without the love and support of my family. Mom, thank you for helping me through the first years of single motherhood. Thank you for your tireless energy and poetic inspiration. For my father, you have always wanted to hear my stories and instilled in me a love of writing and story telling. Harvey and Natasha, thank you for the love and time you have given—especially to Asha. I am grateful to Ishmael Reed, my publisher, for believing in me and in my work. My deepest thanks to Carla Reed, my editor, for her hours upon hours of time helping me define my style. Thank you Joyce Lu, Allison Francis, Kateri and Wally Inglis for your loving readings and edits. Thanks also to Kamau and Asha, loves of my life, inspiration and source of my deepest thankfulness. A sustaining core of women friends kept me going along the way: Lorraine Palumbo, Micheline Soong, Marie Hara, Opal Palmer-Adisa, Kathy Sloane, Amahra Hicks, Herstories Women, Cindy Siok, Audrey Driver, Ailene Romero. Also thank to the guys, Azibuike, Abdi, Macheo, Sean, (the three men and a baby).

Part I

Muse

inspired by the muse of his laughter
she spun rainbows of light
down windy beaches
in mist of night
touched herself
and left herself open
for him to discover

He Said . . . She Said

Woman
wants him to
love her
like he once did,
but he was pretending.

Man
one step ahead
wants her to
love him
the way only a girl can,
after he has made her a woman.

Pussy Controller

She holds the strings to his purse
in her clit
pulling him with universal force.
He leans towards her
then resists.
Flesh tears
through her torso
severing
life chords.

She wonders
how long
can she hold on
to him—
How much power
she really has?

Questioning makes her
weak
in his eyes.

When he entered her
magical cave
he had no idea he
would accidentally drop
his seed
growing vines of entanglements
connecting them forever.

She wants something
he cannot give
money, jewels, seeds
anything
to fill the place
he left
damaged
in poor repair
nothing like he found it.

She is the Pussy Controller
checking credits and debits
keeping tabs on
ins and outs
increases and decreases
in affection.

Measuring love for favors
tone and energy with
devotion and dollars.

So far she has given more
of everything.
He has only taken.

Now he wants to cut that last string.
She resists.
Fighting with all her might
the Royal Cunt
stuns him with a decree:
All submission will cease.
She will control the goods.

He no longer cares.
He has taken what he needs.

I Have Nowhere to put this Sorrow

sunlight rests on green leaves
I sit endlessly
repeating
I need you here
now

Naked to the Party

naked she came
legs long and open
minded people would
not judge her
naked in her
deep cut
paper thin
nipples ripe
floor length
underwearless
evening gown

why did she come
naked
to the party
when she knew
it was for me
that woman
who smiled at me
but was still taking my man

I tend his child, while
she dances on my clean floor

crowning her place
she kisses him—
under my gaze
she kisses me—
apologetically
she out the door—
to return later
to lay in the same bed
where our daughter
lay sleeping
to take my place
and shed her thin
thin costume

Hate = Love (in rhyme)

Your eyes make me sick
pictures of you make me cry
I can't believe everything
you told me was one big lie

Food that you ate makes me
lose my appetite
things that you hate
bring me delight

Our years together
seem like a big waste
except for our daughter
whom our love encased

How can I love her so much
when she is half of you
I want to forget that
but her eyes tell me it's true

She has your frown
your oppressive stare
she has both our color
and both our hair

She loves you so much
So I must keep up this act
I cannot say how I feel
I must not say facts

This torture is for her sake
or is it for mine
I hate you
I hate you
I hate you

Sublime.

Love = Hate (or silence wins)

You come into my room
and stare at me
I talk
you say nothing
I keep talking
you keep silent
finally you win
your silence is louder
I am forced quiet

Your face relaxes
the tension disappears
you have won the battle—
nothing is solved

I rise
shoulders slumped
feet cold
silently mocked
not heard
you are the master
in my house

I hate you
as a slave would

I hide my writing from you
my thoughts
my life

Even on the phone
from 2000 miles
your silence wins

I have nothing left to say to you.

Money

I need it
yes, I want it from you
daddy of my child
my ex-sugar pie,
candy man
lover and friend
it's money I want now
and that's all I want from you
I will not lie
I don't want kindness
I don't want pity
I don't even want to say hi
when you call on the phone
I just want the green
the cash, the bucks
send us some damn money!!!!!!!!

Welfare Queen

What?

you think she doesn't need money?
I know
you think I buy
diamonds and pearls
a welfare queen
scheming to get that extra $64 a month

Well you must have forgotten
how much diapers cost

Already.

Money is the only way
you can show me you care

Yes, send love
in the form of a check

Help me pay for day care
because without your support
I have to work two jobs
and then neither of us will
see our daughter

Help me love her
send money

She'll get love.

Black Woman's Dilemma

Now that I got you out of the way
I can get back to work
more papers to grade
grants to write
countries to save
I can continue
to win awards
and place them on my
dusty shelf
I can share my successes
with my computer
my journal
I can take myself out for a drink or three
have a great time celebrating

Now that I don't have to worry
about you loving me
or wanting to see me
I can spend more time on
me
I can stay up till three in the morning
achieving more things
to brag about to the next man
who will come
then go

Maybe I can practice
my fake orgasm
or write a list
of all the men who have come
and gone

Now that you have set your priorities
I fall at the bottom of your list
I can take you off the top of mine.

No Time for Cafés

In silence of night I write
thoughts cause a stir
in the peace of my child's sleep
she feels me thinking
she misses you the way I do
I love you the way she does

You are always on my mind
while she is constantly
at my feet
hanging on my dress
sleeping in my bed
eating off my plate

I thought I hated you
that you could wrong me no more
but while she and I are alone
together
in this small room
I try to figure out our lives
I still love you
I want to be near you
father of our daughter

I do not want to do this alone.

Swallowing Watermelons

Swallowing whole watermelons of sorrow
breaths come shallow
like one no longer
dependent upon the earth to give her breath.
Grasping but not reaching
through tangles of telephone wire
I am beholden,
our child a lifeline to you.
Invisible cords of communication,
forever linked by her birth.
I am you now
you are me now
she is us.

Resurrection I

dynamic
pussy glowing
mind fucking
man hunting
dominating
angry
daughter of a bitch
just like her mother
coming to get her revenge
on you

Resurrection II

when I come back god
let me remember who I once was
who I wanted to be
which is really
who I once was

Part II

Orgasm in Haiku

sun hot between legs
blessings from earth goddesses
showering manna

Peaches

Your Georgia Peachtree Street accent
dangles from the ends of a word
like ripe fruit I try to taste
on the branches of your tongue.

I swallow your lies because
they are sweet like peach juice
and they run longer than the Mississippi River
into the stream of my blood.

Words from our history
I unconsciously devour
as we park at the river side
and listen to the hum of the crickets.

With you there is always a sunset,
always candy colored sky.
Peach flavored clouds float by
and surround me with the lies
I want to believe because they tell me
that you love me, love that makes you
beautiful. For the slaves of love,
what is false is safe.

Your peach colored love
is like a watercolor, faded.
But I will dance with you
while my heart races in the windy heat
of summer
longing on the Mississippi
for more fruit to eat.

To Be a Man

To be a man
is to be as strong as
a wave breaking over
a bed of lava
cooling Pele's wrathful flames

And as gentle as the ripples
in the tide that cause the mouths
of the sea anemone to sway
without closing

Biking the Bay

sometimes I wonder
what you were thinking
trying to balance on one wheel
on a slab of cement
in the middle of the bay
I wonder what you were thinking
when you walked into the Hilton
clothes soaking wet
to ask me for a hug
in my suit and stockings
you told me that
your bike had fallen
into the blue of the Pacific
and that tomorrow you were
going to ride out
with a dreadlocked brother
in a tiny motor boat to retrieve it
and might you borrow $60 please
sometimes I miss you

Sweet Talker

She's snoring down the street
in red lioness prowl
eyes focused on
what's behind her
she bumps into fate
who knocks her upside her head
hurls her into
portal of passion

Memoirs (self-restraint of a fallen virgin)

i am near him
his breath
we both know
it could happen again
it could
happen that
i kiss him
and touch
his hard
brown breasts
and taste them with my desire
my tongue
my body
could rise up
to meet his again
and he could respond
i know he would

we would wake up
frenzied
questioning
what about him? her?
the others
the children
what about us?

then we would turn
on each other
but he would beg
to stay
but i would make him
leave
i would not even
let him hold my warm
body
still steaming

i would say
you'd better sleep
on that cold couch
or leave now
because if you stay
one more minute
i may fall in love
and then anything could happen
you would not want
to be around for the aftermath

so i kick him out
and sleep alone
holding myself
shivering with cool
satisfaction
no
we know it could happen again
after an evening
of fine conversation

a dinner in a restaurant
with low ceilings
a glass of honey wine
but we won't let it
so we never go inside
we stay on the streets
where it is safe

but in the car
i begin to fall
as he places
a hand so near
i stop driving
we kiss and
my mind says stop
but my body
is a dragon
awakened from its slumber
i am hungry and on fire

he is hot and breathing hard
it is his breath on my neck
if i fall in love with anything
it will be that
and his tender way of talking to me

so i this virgin
am still bound
tied to the tradition
of falling in love
with that man
who breaks my waters

i am falling
like a waterfall
and even here
in the car
with windows steamed
with doors locked
with hands in each other's pockets
even here
i am practicing restraint
when he leaves the car
i am relieved
still a virgin tonight
i watch my knight
disappear into the blackness
of the unknown place that is his home

Lips

You have such big beautiful lips
they make me wanna scream

give me a taste of them lips
before you take them away—lips
be you ti full

how I shiver when they taste mine
I struggle not to identify
with them big beauties
soft, sweet, ice cream lips
dripping with honey, dream lips
sucking me into your world
drawing me in with those beautifullllips

pretending you don't see them
your precocious lips—jutting out
pouting, getting their way with me

can I crawl inside of you?
down your throat, and see what is you?
be you ti full you,
lips that shine in the morning light
I want to touch with my
fingers, hands, nose
mouth, thighs

ears
legs
breasts
your beautifull lips
my lips are in love
agony for the sound of your heart—lips
love
lips
love your big beautifull lips
make me spell all wrong
be you ti full.

Eating a Tomato

(for N.)

her mouth almost touched
mine through red softness of sweet fruit
shivers, aching, lust

Part III

Red Haired Sister in Full Fury

(September 1999)

Again,
my red haired sister
in full fury
beating me down
with anger
she scratches my insides
tears at me
weakening me with loss of
blood

every time I
start to get my self together
full moon shows up
here you are
my enemy
my fertility
the one who can
cause me to create or destroy
myself

I hate her this dragon
queen
her sweet wine scent
her voice of impunity
hers is the only time I am
allowed to show anger.

Red Haired Sister—My Beloved

(October 1999)

Here she is once more
my beloved
assurance that I am
not with child
assurance
that I am still
able to have a child
my inspiration
creative power
my totem
she is my breath
my release
my sigh of many thanks
my prayer
at the end of the month.

The Last Time I Cried

She almighty Faith came
from fire/ice
oblivion
smiling beautiful
Jellomelody
she joined us
brought hope
her radiant peace
to our house
smiling sunflower
a she bubble
it was crazy
the agony through
which she came
vertigo wind
no more solitude
respect burst
I angry
with love
she radiant peace
he smiling ice
what? love
hug me
abstain.

Epilepsy

I hear voices.
Words loud and getting louder.
Your lips move
Sounds repeating,
Like birdcalls.
I don't understand.
My mouth won't answer.
My ears strain to listen.

I see you standing
in front of me, pink face
illuminated by fluorescent
hospital lights,
but I walk into a wall
a chair
any object that obstructs
me in the over familiar passageway.
Then sight turns dark
and I see no more.

I am aware of my muscles twitching,
strong, a runner by nature,
but my legs collapse
beneath me,
and bathroom tiles
imprint on my face.
I am being swallowed by the floor.

I am conscious
just long enough to know
but not enough to stop
and I crash
into unidentified
blackness.

After the First Seizure

Consciousness
something big had happened
and it was bad
but not knowing what
I wanted to be
totally helpless
unconscious
still
to hide from the
eyes of the entire 5th/6th grade class
worried
mocking
frightened
disgusted
they knew this would happen
ever since the first shrill
peacock like sounds
came uncontrollable from my mouth
at first they thought it was a cool joke
that I was cool
then they stopped mentioning it all together
except for the class clown
who stood
mouth finally closed
looking

I
aware of all these
feelings
fear
worry
shame
disgust

Can you stand?
asked the principal
I must have said yes
although I meant no
because he dragged me
to the nurse's office
the ground
treacherously near to my
face
world swirling
as I kept trying to stand
falling
back down
fighting the principal's
grip
one arm up
why didn't he carry me
I wondered?
fear
worry
disgust
and where was my mother?

"Let me goooooooooooo!!!!!"
I screamed
it felt so good to scream at him
my pal
dragging my
eleven year old body
along the cement path
not on the shorter worn
grassy path
past every classroom
so I kept screaming
until we reached the nurse's
office where I slept
until Christmas which is my
next memory.

Car Accident

Awake
I struggle to sit up
but cannot

There is an angel
she is white and glowing
and she is holding
onto my shoulders
restraining me

I see the empty passenger's seat
and I know that I have
killed my sister
whom I all of a sudden remember

I am screaming
let me go let me go
but the angel won't
she keeps holding me down
suddenly I know
I have had a seizure
I have known that all along
that's what happens
when I have seizures
I know they are happening
but I have no control
I must accept it

How can I accept this one?
driving?
with my baby sister in the car
where is she
I am still screaming
where is my sister
time is passing
the angel is holding me down
red lights are flashing everywhere
my sister must have heard me
because she walks by the window
a shadow shrouded in
crimson glow

I stop screaming
stop kicking at the angel
who now asks
if I'm okay
and I wonder
am I?

Then why the hell
is she holding me down
I must have lost my damn legs
or something
I begin to scream again

Then this cop's head
comes through the window
have you been drinking
he interrogates

no
I had a seizure I say
(and I don't have on that dorkey bracelet
because I am only 17 and a cool 17 at that)

Of course he doesn't believe me
—the pig—
he insists I take some sort of test
the angel is still restraining me
now she is saying
you are okay you are okay
the ambulance people thank her
tell her what an angel she is

Can I move?
well if she'd let me go, we'd be
able to find out now wouldn't we
maybe it's anger at the loss of control

I stand
the cops ask me again
if I have been drinking
not tonight I think
I had a damn seizure I say
the pig says yeah right
you could have killed your sister

I am being led to the ambulance
but I decide to start screaming again
because I hate all of them
and I hate myself

Fuck you asshole
I am not going to the damn hospital
then I realize
I was driving my mother's new car
(through an intersection into a stoplight
they whisper on the sidelines
and then she backed into the wall
we were sure she was a goner . . .
so lucky . . .)

Fuck
the angel has one arm
and the cop has the other
they are leading me by force
heels pressed to the ground
to the ambulance
I totaled my mom's new car
she is going to kill me

My mother arrives
she is panicked
my sister is in the cop car
are you mad Mom?

Sorry about the car
I really am
I'm so sorry
I cannot stop saying it
I am sorry
I am sorry
am sorry
so sorry
so so sorry

Damn fucking epilepsy
fucking brain
fucking self

At the ambulance
the pig asks me
again
if I have been drinking
my mother tells him I have epilepsy
she asks where the dorky bracelet is
which you all know the story of
the cop says yeah right
we'll see about that

I lay back
they restrain me again
it's procedure they say
to have to lay back
in the weird car bed
with restraints on
mom can ride with me
dad will follow in his car with my sis

I don't want to go to the damn hospital
can't you see I'm okay
this happens to me all the time
on the bus
on the street
in the library
in my bed

This is just my life!

Part IV

Premonition

Her mother
is going
to kill some body
some day

she can feel it coming

and

if
no
one
else

it
is
going
to
be
her.

Competition of the Hair

Did it start with the lie of the hair?
that the big round kinky
was somehow not equal to the
straight shiny silky

was there some reason why her frizzy black
did not compare
to my long flowing
bleached by the sun
uncombed for the ragged effect
honey tresses

all of that head flapping
neck twirling
wrist flipping
arms sashaying potential
that I had
she did not

who insisted she wear it under a hat?
cover over that "shameful nappy"
straighten, dye, braid, cut
mangle anything but face
the mirror
of who we are

different black faces
one dark the other less
one curled the other straight
teeth and nose
chin and eyes
shaped by ancestors
some common, others lost
each wishing to be what she is not

the child to be curled like her mother
the mother to be straight like her mother before
alternating generations of light and dark
genes
is this the lie of the hair
the truth of unacceptance.

Breasts

Your breasts are shriveled.
That's the only difference
between us.
Otherwise
We could be
would be
sisters.

But I sucked
your milk
your breasts
your youth.

Now as you
watch me dress
you ask where your
breasts went.

Telling me I have
full
round
supple
breasts
like you used to have.

I did not steal them—
no.
You did not give them—
a gift.
You sacrificed them—
for me.

Great Grandmother Maud

hanging clothes in the summer
that's how I remember her
white sheets
yellow
sun
hot Alabama
shining
beating down on her
disguised behind
a celebrating sky
symphony of clouds
lemonade
and southern hospitality

they are billowing
in the breeze
starched and white
she is
in an apron
it is white
and her dress is yellow
her long black hair is pulled back into a bun
but it keeps slipping out
and she
uses her free hand to brush it back
hair
sheets
white

black
billowing
she hums a love song
Dinah Washington
hums to herself as she remembers
not her children
or her job
not her husband

but she remembers
last night
the sweetest shadow
the slightest sound
and the deepest pleasure
in between these same sheets
which she is washing only because
the evidence must be hidden
her man
not the first or
even her second
he is the young one
fiery and lovely
from across the way
he is the one who is really going someplace
his skin is as black
as the Alabama sky is blue
and his kisses are so hot that she shivers in
the relentless sun
she is humming a tune
that only a lady who flirts with death
knows how to sing

and that is how I first remember her.

the next memory is of her
dead
there on those same sheets
laying on the ground with the laundry basket
still on her hip as if stuck
blood staining the sheets
red evidence of passing
her throat is slit
and her life
seeps away into the ground in shame
a no good woman
left to be remembered by no one
this is my great grandmother
the woman no one spoke of for years
the woman who
marked the beginning
of what
I don't know

Wanna Be White Girl

I was a white girl once
who dreamed of riding a Harley Davidson
and drinking vodka straight
while leaning over a pool table
tattoo on my ankle
that said property of . . .

I was a white girl
who had white friends
and white boyfriends
who loved me and
drank with me
locked me in closets
told racial jokes
then apologized

We drank gin and tonic
and roamed the streets
looking for trouble
because it never did seem to come to us

I was white
yes
I was white
and I wore torn blue jeans and tie dye
I listened to the Rolling Stones
and Lynard Skynard
I lived the words and knew the pain they held

When I was white I dreamed of being

Old Home's Day Queen
at the county fair
where music was real
and women wore cowboy boots
I had my Stetson and my
Buck knife

I danced the two-step
and played Bingo on Saturday nights

When I was white I loved a man
named Cincinnatuss who drove a Harley
flew colors, and lived in West Virginia
we drank every type of liquor all
mixed up into one
we danced to country music
and fell out the door when it was time to go
when we fought
it was violent
but I loved him like I have never loved

I rode in fast cars listening to The Who
asking "*who are you?*"

But I was white
I was
I was in on the secrets
the truths the lies
the only problem was
that people kept mistaking me for being
Hawaiian or Chinese
Palestinian
or Black

So I looked in the mirror and saw
my skin is brown
my hair is brown
my eyes are brown
and I wondered
where did God go wrong
because being a white girl
trapped in a black body
is no small mistake
and the stress was beginning to take its toll.

You see even though Van Morrison sang
Brown Eyed Girl
I knew there was more to it than that
because didn't nobody really
seem to want to marry me
and not many people really took
me seriously
and for some reason
I just didn't seem to fit,
older I got—
no matter how much I drank

So, I killed her
I killed that white girl that I once was
I stopped her life
cut it short with one clean swipe
no more Led Zeppelin
no more white boyfriends
no more dreams of making my brown eyes blue

But I was a white girl once
you wouldn't know it by looking
that once dreamed of drinking vodka
straight while laying back on a pool table
tattoo on my ankle that said
property of . . . .

Dating the Oppressor

there are worse things
than dating the oppressor
like beating your child
letting your ex-wife starve
while you enjoy a newer
fancier feast

there are worse things
than loving what
you should not love
like eating dolphin
buying sweatshop shoes

when i look into his blue eyes
i should see the way
his ancestors raped mine
but instead i just see him adoring me
(it has been so long since i was adored)
when he does not tell me i am beautiful
i wonder . . . do i still have it?
maybe i am not so exotic
anymore

there are worse things than this
i know there are
like . . .
well . . .
like eating and then vomiting when others
are starving
and maybe not
maybe i am deceiving myself again . . .

being exotic is so relative

Ogun: New Year's Eve 2000

Ogun is a trickster in the Yoruba tradition

Ogun jumps out of the blaze
into the body of my mother
doing a flaming war dance

a bon of fire works
lights the yard
wrapped in black velvet
she bursts out of the shadow
braids flying
streaking the night
in motion

with hands crisscrossing
over knees
she revives
a dance of her youth—
her mother's youth—
a girl again

I see her hopes and dreams
basement parties
spiked punch
the Temptations
slow dancing in the dark

as laughter masks our faces
I want so badly to
say that I love her
and that I forgive her
for anything that I
may have been angry at
still

then as quickly as
the shadow of her youth
Ogun disappeared
and she became
the woman
I have always known.

Womb Dancing

Hair is electric
women move in rhythmic trances
womb dancing
following notes with their hips
stopping drumbeats with their thighs
swallowing entire sections of brass
to exhaust the position
"got soul"
cause they keep getzing it
and birthing it
and raising it higher
than they imagined

Voices come in different shapes
and melt like colors into
choruses of purple
and orange
each moving in and out of each other
like raindrops
while women move
in the warmth of raining notes
of bass beat blues and reds
until the saxophone calls them back
and they float upwards
clouds of color
into the sky
gathering old spirits and
giving them new life.

Asha

According to one Yoruba language dictionary,
Asha means "Life," and in another, it means "Amen."
I've also been told that in Hindi, it means "Hope."

Can you push again?
hell yeah
and I did
out past my vagina
past the pain
where she lay
in the ring of fire
helping me
pushing too
for her life
hard
labor
panting
screaming
groaning
needing everybody there to help me
and you
Asha
life
hope
I wanted you so bad
it didn't matter if it hurt

what was pain?
can you push again?
hell yeah
hold on baby
you are coming out
now
hurt?

Did it hurt
no
not like the pain
I can only imagine
if someone
tried to take her away
not like the stabbing pain that
would be your blood
if you hurt her

Asha, I never want you to hurt
never
but I know it is impossible
unfair for me to protect you
I never knew it could hurt so much
to love so much

Can you push again
hell yeah
and I did.

Getting Ready for the Worst

car accidents
tornadoes
telephone electrocutions
plane crashes
drug addiction
reckless teenage years
pregnancy
giving up
getting lost in cyberspace
unfulfilled dreams
not being prepared for the future
(no more good night kisses
sweet laughs)
scars
falling out of trees
sky falling
drowning
molestation
losing faith in men
losing faith in mom

(no more good-bye kisses
or sweet voice)
being run over by an elephant
having a coconut fall on her head
rape
disfigurement
scarification
no more beautiful
perfect child
is this about me
or her

He Said

(for him)

He said you are too melodramatic
so I stopped crying.

He said you are too abstract
but he was lying.

He said be more concrete
because he couldn't understand.

He said how are you doing
without really asking.

He said for me to love him
I was doing all I could.

He said can't you be more honest
so I wrote a poem for him.

Whore She Is (Not)

She welcomes him
in the back door with two
bottles of cheap green beer
he takes her hand
and they fall
together on the bed

clothes off
before the door is shut
no matter that
they have not spoken for months
when he calls
(girl get a baby sitter
I am coming over)
she knows what he means
and she does
and he does
come

over
he says for the
one hundredth time
I am not the kind of man
for you
you are a nice girl and
you want more than I
could ever give you

skin to skin
she tries to kiss
his neck he pulls away
don't mark me
he says
and she laughs
I am not your
whore

but he knows
she loves it
when he takes her
by surprise
forces her
on to the bed
refuses to acknowledge
her needs
she wants him
to push her down
to overpower her
and most of all
she wants him to leave
when he is finished.

Whore'song

Accepting what is hers
she folds her napkin
and places the last of her
coins on the table
next to her fork

Satan,
horned and ready for battle,
retreats.

Expecting Heaven

I was expecting heaven
and it fell from the sky
clouded my vision
white and misty
so bright at times
I was blinded

It walked in my door
offering itself
it was not enough

Take all of me
he said
but I refused

When he held me
I only thought about
when he would
leave

His energy
went right through

leaving me
unchanged
and alone

I demanded to be paid back
for the time I had
wasted in heaven
changed my story
said it was hell
refused to take the blame
for wanting too much and
accepting nothing
I was expecting hell
and it won't ever come
life keeps me alive
pushing against negative
fiery thoughts
when he left me
I blamed him
though I ran away
took all that he had

I protected myself.

Peas in a Pod

one late night journey to dreamland
two peas in a pod lay sleeping
she reaches out
caressing him
gently into wakefulness
dreaming of girlhood
and candy cane days
hot and sticky in her hand
she wakes
to his hardness
but knows not where she is or why
feeling the contradiction of
time flying
she cries out
I am a mother now!
as if to remind herself
he hears her
and places his hand
where she likes to be comforted
wet
she is ashamed
that he does not see
the little girl
still in her dreams
watching herself become a woman

Salt and Black Pepper

i am salt
and black pepper
i am collard greens with fat back
cooked and re-cooked
for three days
at least

i am steamed white rice
eaten every evening
with fork
not chopstick

i am apple pie
cinnamon and sugar
cooked in pure fruit juice
covered with flaky crust
and baked
until i'm done

i am
repeat after me
i am
proud to be who i am
mama
an' i don't care what
other kids say

said
i am from the country
i am from the country

when my mind rambles
i follow a path
over squished strawberry guavas
through bamboo forest
down the gully
to the river where we used to bathe

when i remember
i hear bob marley
singin' *stir it up*
but we brown people
be sittin' stoned
jus' listenin'
not movin'

i see tadpoles
me walkin'
barefoot
through knee-deep mud puddles
to get to school
hoping only that
they will not dry up
before 3:00
so i can swim on my way home

i smell the fragrance of fresh
picked plumeria
pikake
puakenikeni
gardenia
all together
overshadowed by my mother's
strong perfume

i smell fried chicken
and roses
greens
and the sticky air
of rice steaming

i, yes, i
i am from the country
and i surprise myself to say it
but i am a country girl

my father catches rain water
on the roof of his house
in an old water bed frame
for us to drink and bathe in
at night there are mosquitoes

my mother catches big yellow and black
garden spiders in a glass jar
to spread in her garden
but still there are mosquitoes

i was never proud to be this
i was never proud
but i am a daughter
of thousands of years
of daughtering
now i am a mother
and i pass on to my daughter
all my traits
good and bad
so that she can take what she needs
and improve upon my faults

i am doing the best i can
like a flower in a sidewalk crack
a bird of paradise
growing in cement
not out of choice
but because i have roots here
and since i am here now
i hope that people who pass
stop to see
the color amongst the grey
texture in the monotony
softness thriving
within hardness

To Set Me Free

She is the goddess of laughter
carefully wrapped in silk scarves
a golden crown

her skin fresh and soft
like the first time
I kissed her
felt laughter welling up
deep in my womb
from which she had just come

Laughter
she brought me
from that other place
laughter I had lost
in carrying watermelons
through bamboo forests
of what ifs?

She answered with
knock knock

Who's there?

Goddess

Goddess who?

Goddess of laughter.

About the author

Karla Brundage was born in Berkeley, California, in the 1967 Summer of Love. She is a poet, essayist, writer, activist, performer, and teacher. Her poetry has been published in various literary journals and magazines including: *Bamboo Ridge*, *Konch*, *Hip Mama*, *Oahu Review*, *Kaimana*, and *La'iLa'i*. Her poetry has been included in the anthologies *Intersecting Circles: Voices of Hapa Women in Poetry and Prose* (Bamboo Ridge Press, 1999) and *Adam of Ife: Black Women in Praise of Black Men* (Lotus Press, 1992). Her essays have appeared in the journal *Bamboo Ridge*, and in the anthologies *Multi-America: Essays on Cultural Wars and Cultural Peace*, edited by Ishmael Reed (Viking Press, 1997) and *Conversations: Essays for Reading and Writing* (Longman, 2003). Her writing has been performed in stage productions including *The Medea Project*, directed by Rhodessa Jones (San Francisco Center for the Arts, 1994); *Carving Circles* directed by Joyce Lu (Earl Ernst Lab Theater, May,1997); and *The Herstories Project,* directed by Emily Burkes-Nossiter (Exit Theater, 2005).

Karla Brundage has read her poetry in New York at such venues as the Nuyorican Poets Café and Vassar College. As a young artist, she worked on a number of collaborative performance pieces with San Francisco Bay area dancers and musicians. In the early 90's, she participated in the Bay area's open mic revival, which fused poetry and music during the early days of Hip-Hop. She read at Mr. 5's, 848 Divisadero, Small Press Traffic, La Peña, and the Women's Building. In Hawaii in the late 90's, she was again on the forefront of a poetry renaissance, as a featured reader at open mics all over Honolulu, and hosting a number of events and poetry slams. She often read at the University of Hawaii, and with Ishmael Reed at Borders and at Barnes and Noble. Since moving back to Oakland, Karla Brundage has continued to perform at clubs, cafes, galleries, and libraries, at the City of Oakland's Art and Soul Festival, and at the Fall 2004 Annual Conference of the National Council of Teachers of English.

Karla Brundage received a degree in English Literature from Vassar College, where she studied post-colonial African literature with then-exiled South African professor, Dr. Moses Nkondo. In 1999, she received her MA in Education from San Francisco State University, specializing in Multicultural Curriculum Development and Implementation. As a participant in the Fulbright Teacher Exchange Program in 2001, she spent a year teaching in Zimbabwe. Her efforts to effect social change through art include participation in Poetic Protests, and teaching poetry to youths in the penal system as well as to women and men in maximum-security facilities. She currently lives in the San Francisco Bay area, where she teaches creative writing and literature.

BVG